This book belongs to

....

WHAT HALLOWEEN CANDY IS NEVER ON TIME FOR THE PARTY?

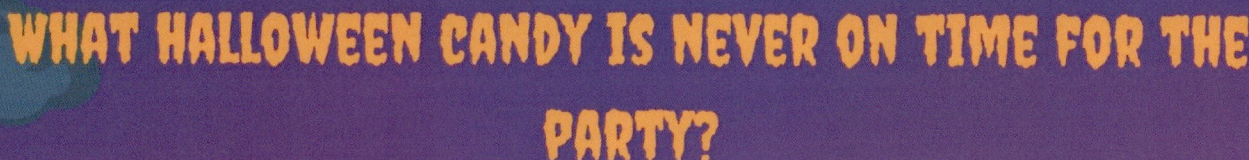

Choco-late!

WHICH HALLOWEEN MONSTER IS GOOD WITH NUMBERS?

Count dracula!

WHY DID THE CYCLOPS GIVE UP TEACHING?

WHERE DOES THE DRACULA KEEP HIS MONEY?

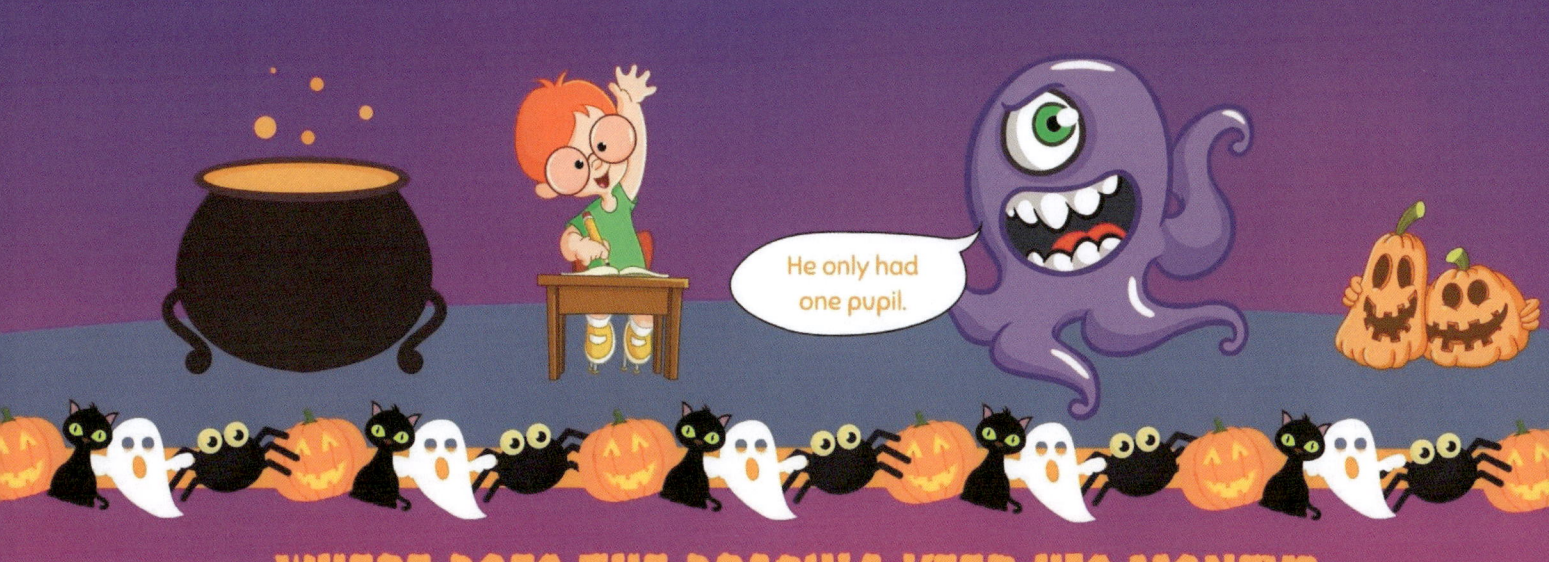

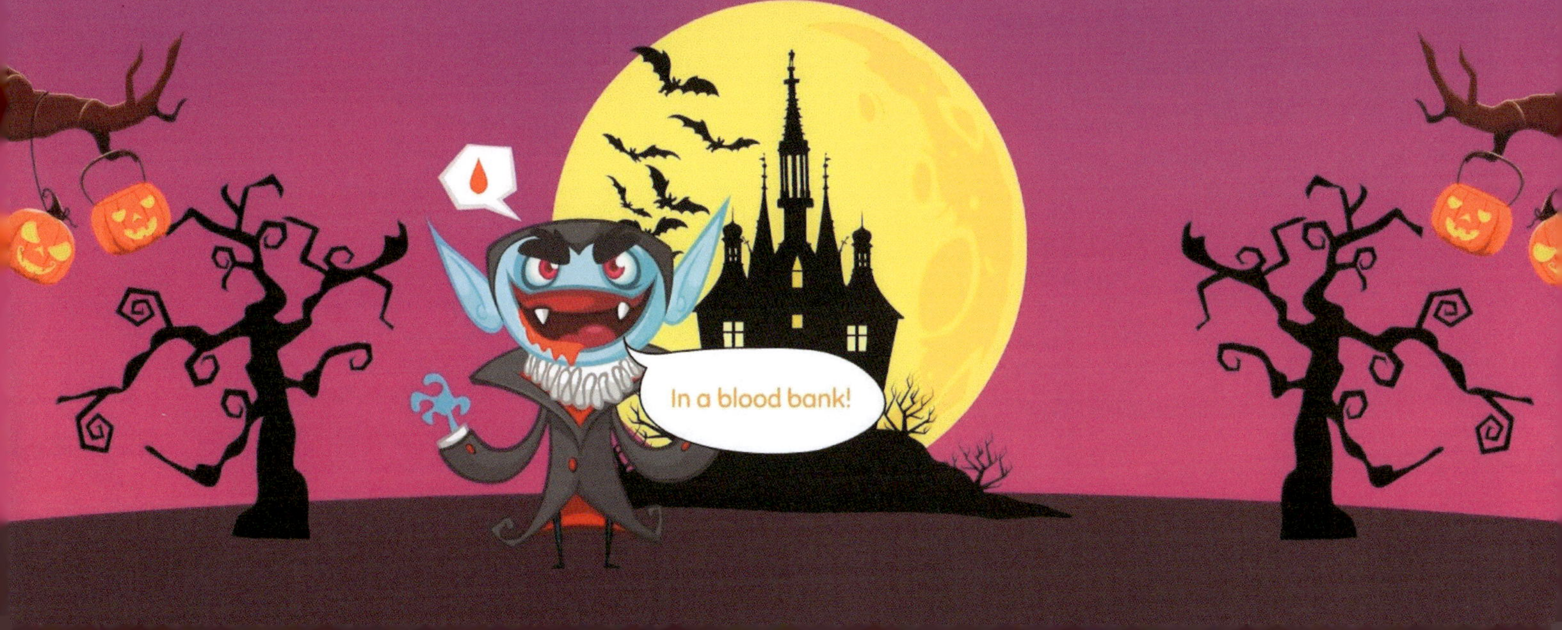

WHAT DOES A PANDA GHOST EAT?

Bam-BOO!

WHERE DO GHOSTS BUY THEIR FOOD?

At the ghost-ery store!

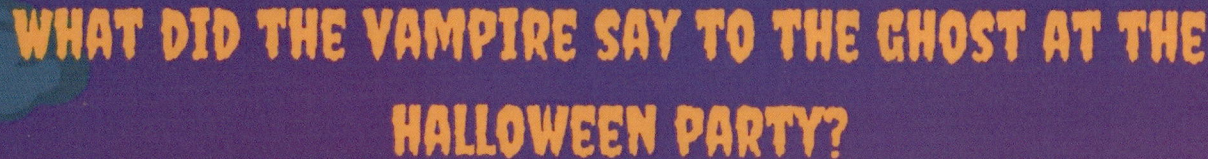

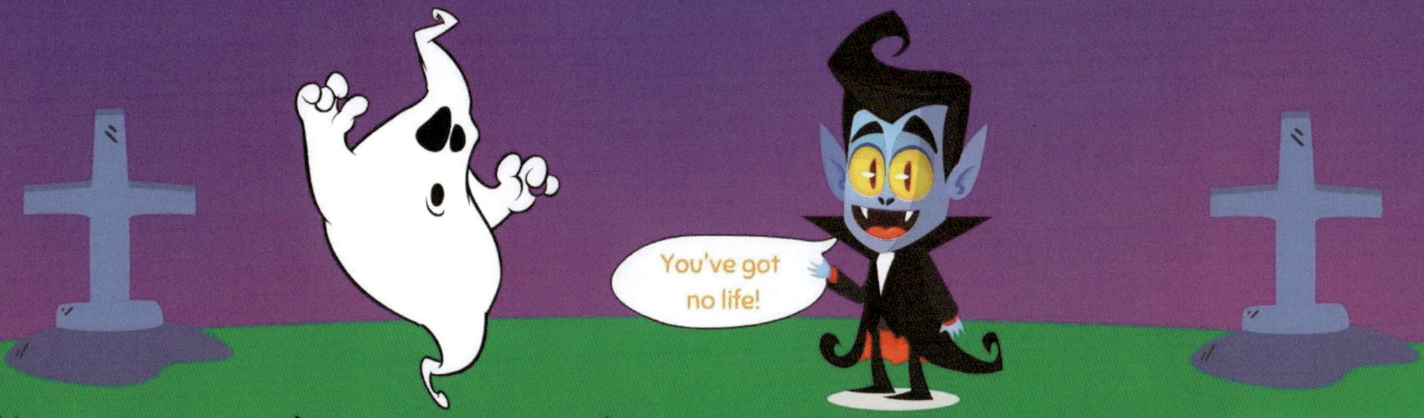

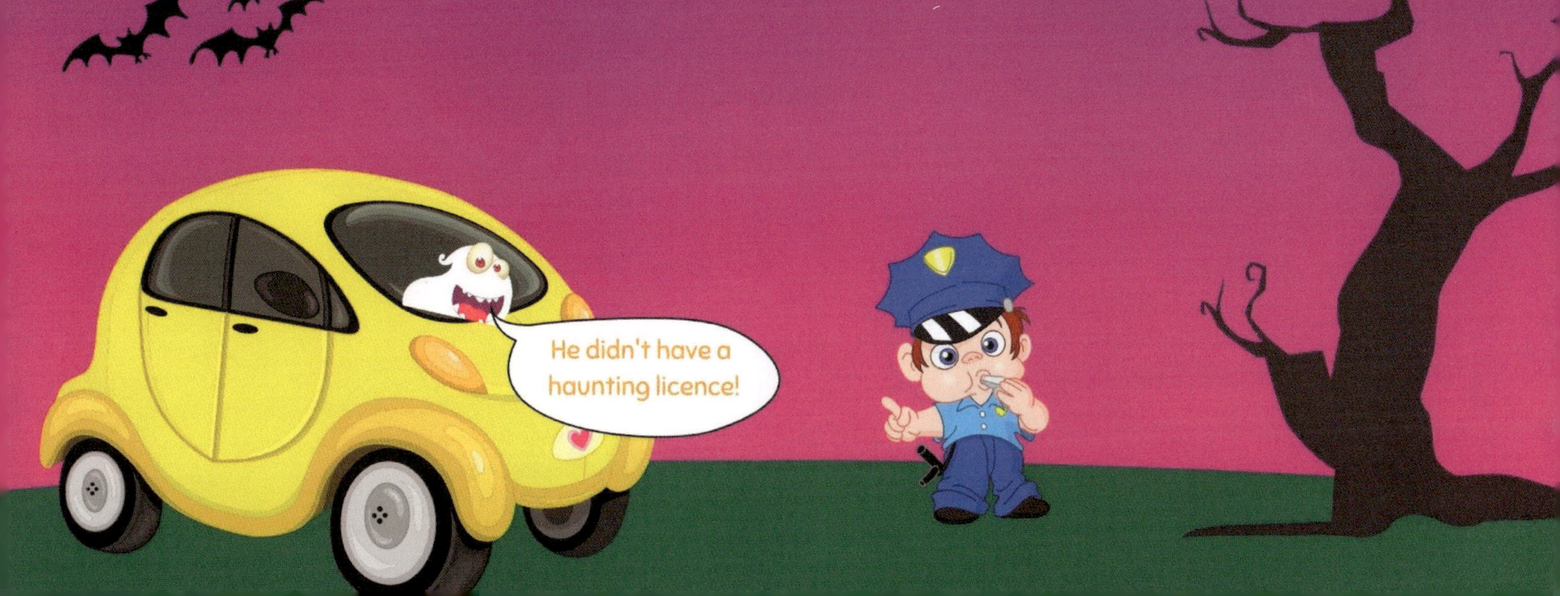

WHAT DAY DO ZOMBIES EAT PEOPLE?

Chewsday!

WHAT DID THE OTHER KIDS THINK ABOUT THE BOY WHO SHOWED UP DRESSED UP AS A MUSHROOM?

They thought he was a fun guy!

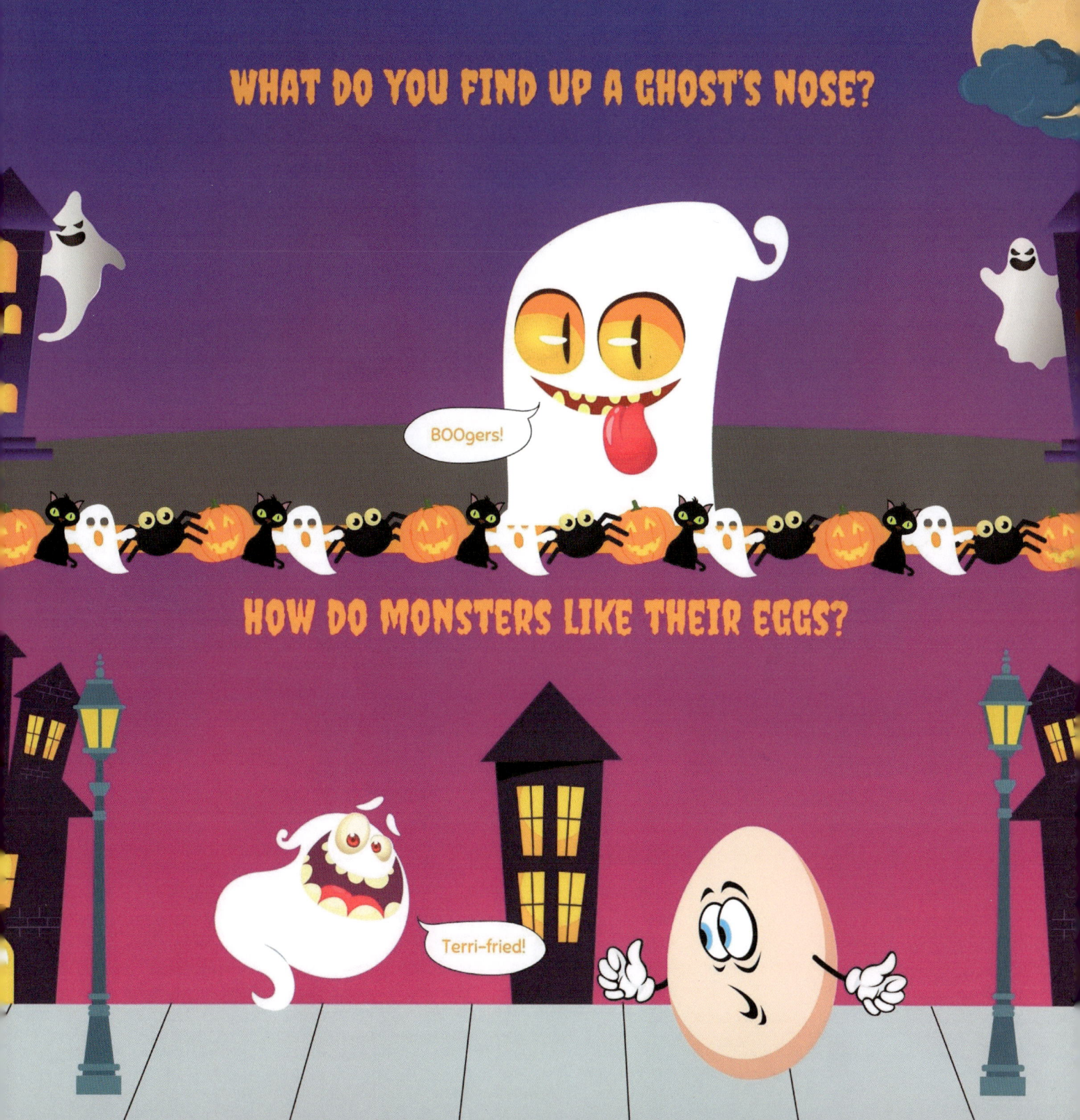

HOW DO YOU MAKE A SKELETON LAUGH?

WHAT FLAVOUR ICE CREAM DO DRACULA'S EAT?

WHAT DO GHOSTS TURN ON IN THE SUMMER?

Scare-conditioner.

HOW CAN YOU TELL IF A VAMPIRE HAS A COLD?

He starts coffin!

WHAT DID THE GHOST'S DO WHEN THEY WHEN TO THE SOCCER GAME?

They booed!

WHAT DO SKELETONS ORDER AT A RESTAURANT?

Spare ribs.

WHAT DO ITALIAN GHOSTS HAVE FOR DINNER?

Boo-ghetti!

WHAT'S A VAMPIRE'S FAVOURITE FRUIT?

Neck-tarine.

WHY DIDN'T THE SKELETON CROSS THE ROAD?

He didn't have any guts!

WHAT TYPE OF TVS ARE IN HAUNTED HOUSES?

Wide scream TVs!

WHAT DO SKELETONS FLY IN?

A scare-plane or a skelecopter!

WHAT IS A SKELETON'S FAVOURITE INSTRUMENT?

A sax-a-bone.

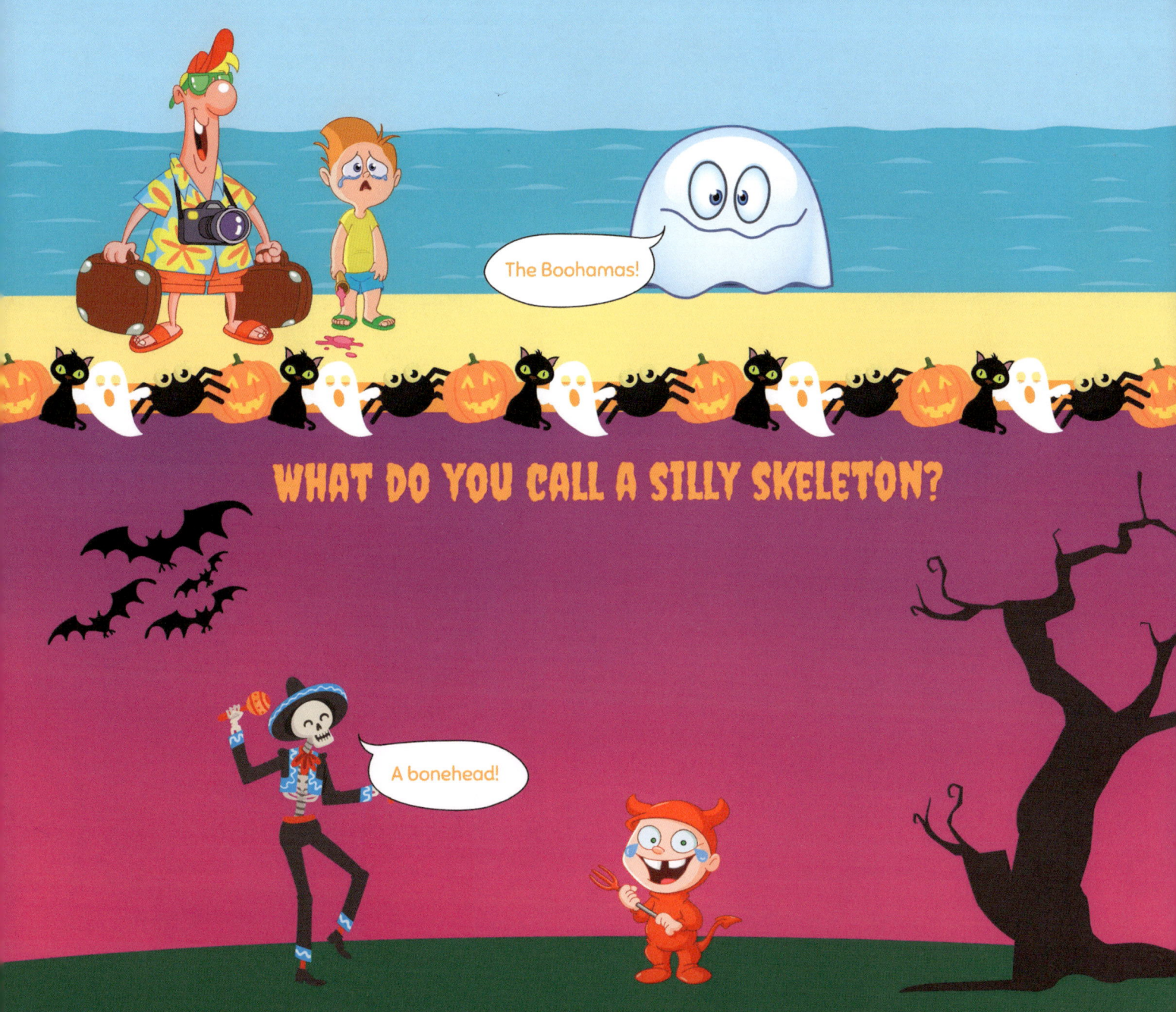

WHAT DO YOU CALL A WITCH WHO GOES TO THE BEACH?

WHAT DO WITCHES RACE ON?

WHY DIDN'T THE SKELETON GO TRICK-OR-TREATING?

He had no body to go with!

WHAT IS A MONSTER'S FAVOURITE DESSERT?

I scream!

ON WHICH DAY ARE GHOSTS MOST SCARY?

Fright-day!

DID YOU HEAR ABOUT THE MONSTER WHO ATE HIS HOUSE?

He was homesick!

HOW DO GHOSTS WASH THEIR HAIR?

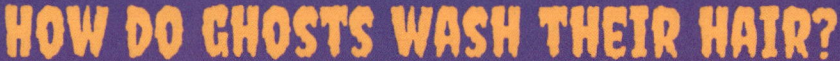

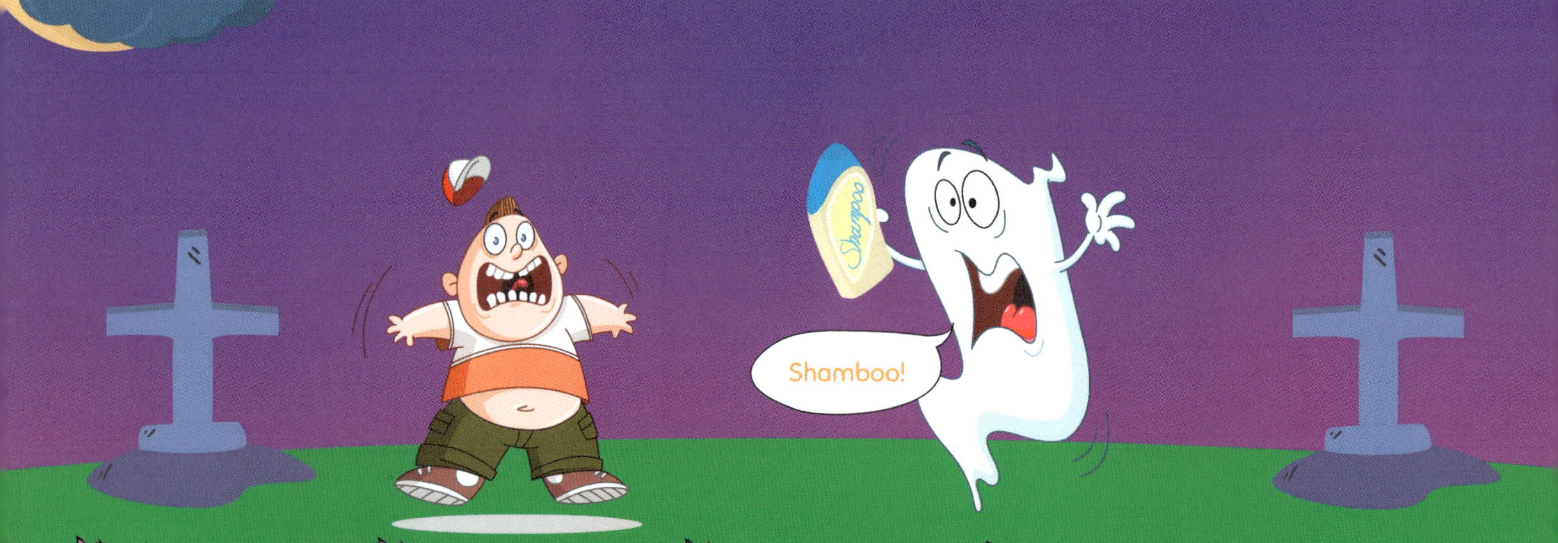

WHAT'S A WITCH'S FAVOURITE SUBJECT IN SCHOOL?

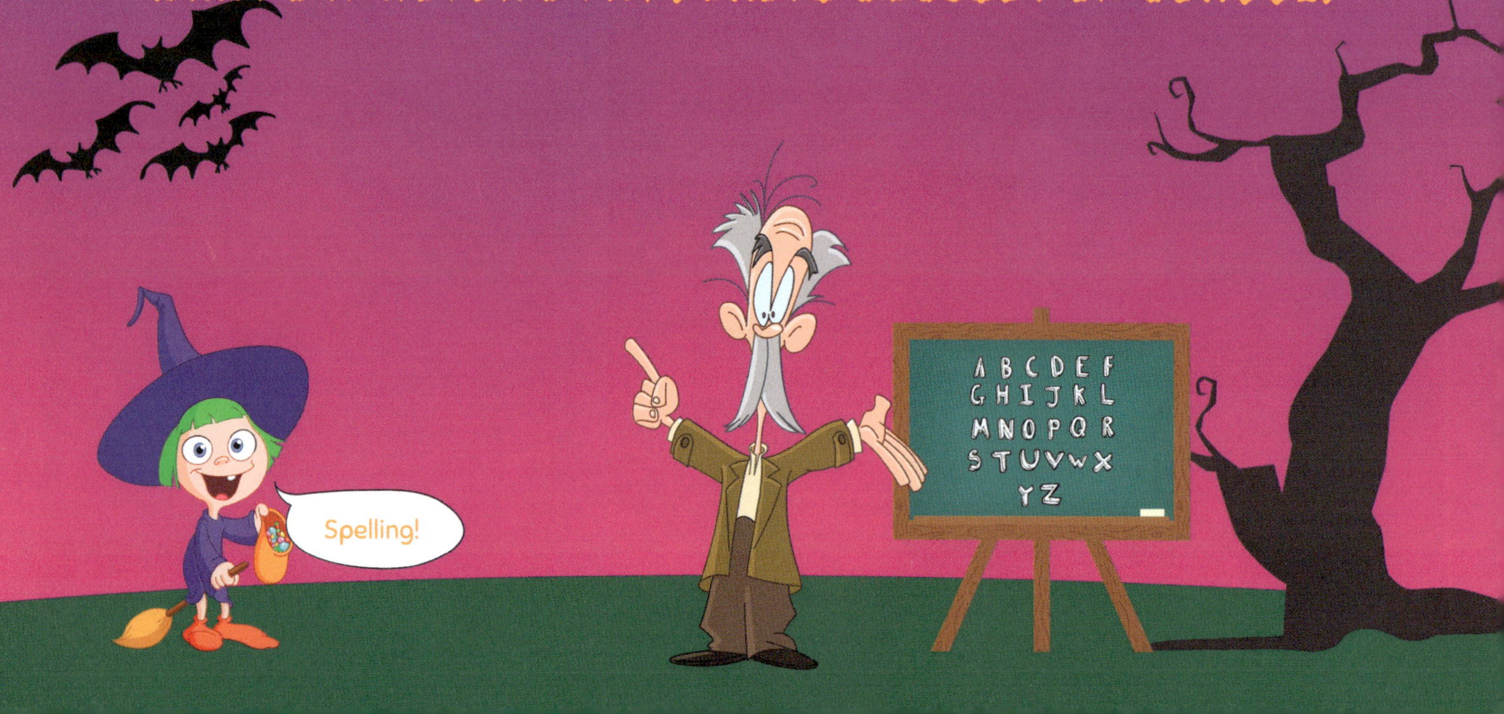

Printed in Great Britain
by Amazon